ALL-TIME GREATS

Renardo Barden

BASKETBALL
HEROES

The Rourke Corporation, Inc.
Vero Beach, Florida 32964

The Rourke Corporation, Inc.
P.O. Box 3328, Vero Beach, FL 32964

Barden, Renardo.
  All time greats / by Renardo Barden.
    p.   cm. — (Basketball heroes)
  Includes bibliographical references and index.
  Summary: Discusses the history of basketball and significant individuals in the sport.
  ISBN 0-86593-163-1
    1. Basketball—United States—History—Juvenile literature. 2. Basketball players—United States—Biography—Juvenile literature. [1. Basketball—History. 2. Basketball players.]
  I. Title. II. Series.
  GV885.7.B315   1992
  796.323—dc20

                                                                92--12053
                                                                CIP
                                                                AC

Series Editor: Gregory Lee
Editor: Marguerite Aronowitz
Book design and production: The Creative Spark, San Clemente, CA
Cover photograph: Stephen Dunn/ALLSPORT

Contents

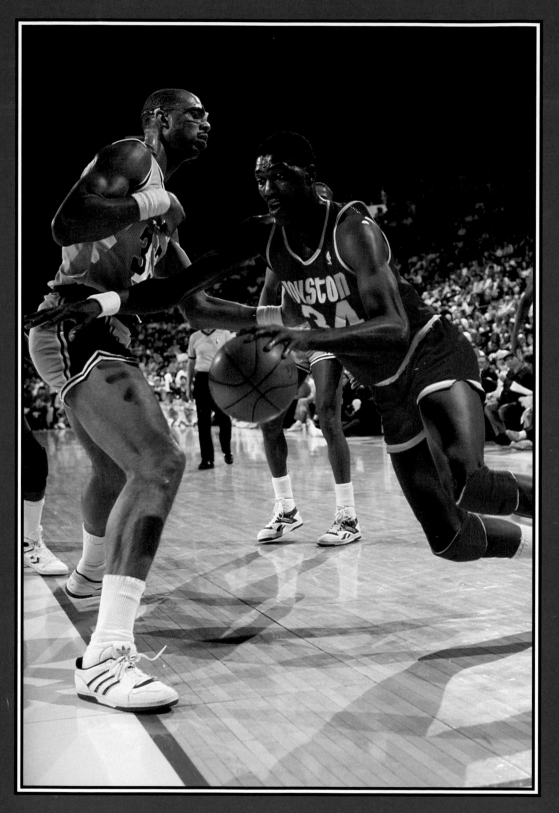

James Naismith, the creator of basketball, would probably not recognize the fast-paced pro game as played by today's NBA stars.

The Birth Of The Game

About 100 years ago, a student in Massachusetts named Frank Mahan was exercising in a gym when he noticed a pair of peach baskets nailed to the overhead running track. When he saw a leather ball lying nearby, he turned to his teacher and scoffed, "Ha, another new game, huh?"

Mahan's coach was James Naismith, a new teacher at the YMCA Training School in Springfield, and he had just written the basic rules for basketball. It was a game that would become one of the most popular participant sports in the world.

Aware that many YMCA students were restless and bored by exercises, Naismith's boss had given him two weeks to come up with something different. Naismith set his sights on a game less violent than rugby—a game without blocking, tackling, or kicking. He hoped to design a game that people of all ages could play. It should be a simple game, he thought, using a medium-sized ball.

Naismith decided on a contest that would call for throwing a ball into a goal. But since he didn't want outdoor rough stuff, he had to solve the problem of preventing players from simply surrounding the goal and blocking attempts to score. He decided to place the goals out of reach.

The Springfield gym had an indoor running track

located ten feet above the gym floor. Naismith nailed peach baskets to the base of the track, and the baskets have remained ten feet from the floor ever since.

Naismith's class was made up of 18 young men, so he divided the class evenly into two teams. Players either passed the ball back and forth, or tried to score by shooting for the basket. Scoring was difficult, particularly since dribbling and running with the ball were against the rules.

The early rules were vague and the equipment crude, but the first players didn't seem to mind. In fact, they enjoyed the new game so much that when they went home for Christmas vacation, they taught it to their friends.

Within a few weeks, Naismith's 13 rules for the new game were published in a YMCA newsletter. The publication of these rules had much the same effect as an outlet pass today to James Worthy or Scottie Pippen. The game of basketball was up and running its own fast break into history.

The first public basketball game took place in Springfield, Massachusets, on March 2, 1892, when the YMCA Training School students played their teachers. The early games might have looked a little crude to those of us who have seen Julius Erving, Charles Barkley, or Michael Jordan, but flashiness had yet to make its way into the sport. Five-player teams, bleachers, electronic scoreboards, free throws, jump shots, three-point shots, and backboards were all in the future.

When Naismith wrote the first rules, he was trying to develop a game for students who didn't like exercising in the gym. He didn't imagine—and no one else did, either—that the game called basketball would grow the way it did, or that players would make so much money.

The Naismith Memorial Basketball Hall of Fame is named for the man who made up the first 13 rules of basketball: James Naismith.

During his later years, Naismith never tired of reminding listeners that he had created a game to be played—not watched. But right from the start, those who couldn't or wouldn't play Naismith's game still found it exciting. To many it provided the perfect indoor outlet for the American spirit of competition. In fact, spectators have had almost as much to do with the history of basketball as the players. For instance, backboards were first used to keep eager fans from blocking shots themselves!

Not long after he wrote the famous 13 rules, Naismith left Massachusets. He became director of physical education at the University of Kansas at Lawrence, where he coached basketball until 1907. Just before he retired in 1936, the National Association of Basketball Coaches raised money so he could attend the Olympics in Berlin, Germany. That was the first time basketball was to be played in the Olympics. Naismith had the honor of tossing up the ball in the first Olympic basketball game between Estonia and France.

When he returned to the United States he proposed that the money he had left over from his trip be set aside for a Basketball Hall of Fame. Unfortunately, early efforts to establish the Hall were delayed by Naismith's death and America's involvement in World War II.

Patrick Ewing has had an impressive career with the New York Knicks, but will he earn a place in the Hall of Fame?

The Hall Is Built

But interest in creating a Hall of Fame lived on. Still lacking the funds for a permanent building, a group calling itself the Basketball Hall of Fame Honors Committee met in 1959 in a little red brick house near the Springfield College football field. There they elected Dr. Naismith as the first member of the Basketball Hall of Fame.

The Naismith Memorial Basketball Hall of Fame was finally dedicated on June 30, 1985. Located on a three-acre site in downtown Springfield, about 70 miles southwest of Boston, it offers visitors 52,000 square feet of exhibits.

Since Naismith always preferred the game of basketball to the sport of basketball, he would no doubt be pleased that the Hall of Fame has chosen to honor many different people associated with the game. The Hall includes many members who gave something important to basketball without ever becoming wealthy or famous in the modern NBA. For example, although women's basketball wasn't played in the Olympics until 1976, females have played the game from its earliest beginnings. Probably nobody did as much to bring women's basketball to the public's attention as Cheryl Miller, who led the 1984 U.S. Olympic team to victory over the Russians.

And then there was Bertha F. Teague, who coached at Ada Byng High School in Ada, Oklahoma. Teague was one of the most successful coaches in basketball history. From 1927 to 1969, her teams won ten games for every game they lost over a period of more than 40 years. She retired in 1969 with a string of 1,152 wins and 115 losses. Her record at state championship tournaments was one that famous coaches such as John Wooden, Red Auerbach, and Bobby Knight could only dream of. She was elected to the Hall in 1985.

George Mikan was one of the best centers in NBA history and became one of the first players elected to the Hall of Fame.

The Hall And Early Greats

Any one can be nominated to the Basketball Hall of Fame. Nominations are made by completing a four-page form and sending it in to the Basketball Hall of Fame Honors Committee. Three letters of recommendation from "outstanding basketball persons" must be submitted with the form. Newspaper and magazine articles about the candidate are also required. At the end of each season, the 24-member committee reviews all applications and holds elections. Current membership in the Hall includes 84 players (51 of whom played in the NBA), 43 coaches, 42 contributors, and 11 referees.

Those who favor basketball as a sport—especially the fans—argue that the Hall of Fame should admit only the best players. They also say that the best players in the world are playing for the NBA, and so the Hall of Fame need only select NBA players. And maybe some coaches, referees, and contributors to the NBA could also be considered.

Other basketball fans, however, note that there is more to basketball than the various ways of measuring who is best. They fear that some of the most talented and interesting people in basketball will be overshadowed if Hall of Fame membership is limited to only established NBA stars.

With recent changes in the way the Hall of Fame

selects its members, it will be interesting to see if the Hall is able to maintain its dedication to the entire game. Perhaps the Basketball Hall of Fame will become like the baseball and football Halls of Fame. But if the Basketball Hall of Fame admits only NBA players with careers spanning many years, much of basketball's history will be forgotten.

George Mikan—Elected 1959

Before becoming modern basketball's first dominant big man at six-feet, ten-inches tall and 250 pounds, George Mikan turned down offers to become a professional baseball pitcher. After graduating from DePaul University where he all but ruled the college backboards, Mikan joined a National Basketball League (NBL) team known as the Chicago American Gears.

In the days before the 24-second shot clock, basketball was still a rough game. Four of Mikan's teeth were knocked out during his debut. Then he quit the Gears after 25 games because of a salary dispute. Things were better for Mikan when he joined the Minneapolis Lakers the following year. For starters, he led the league in scoring. Known for using his elbows and getting his way under the basket, Mikan was an early Bill Laimbeer type—but a better shooter. He was so dominant that in 1952, the rule-makers widened free-throw lanes from six to twelve feet to keep him from controlling the game under the basket.

Big as he was, Mikan was both the target and the source of rough play. During his career he received a total of 166 stitches to close various cuts and wounds, and he broke more than half a dozen bones. Basketball was still a little like prize fighting.

In a poll of 123 coaches taken in 1955, Mikan was named the all-time greatest player of the game. He was slow-footed, however, and it was probably a good thing that he retired shortly after the 24-second shot clock rule made for a faster-paced game (a team has to shoot within 24 seconds after receiving the ball). When he retired in 1956 after nine years of play with a scoring average of 22.6, Laker coach John Kundla said, "Well, at least this should even up the league."

John Wooden—Elected 1960 (player) and 1972 (coach)

A high school basketball star in the 1920s, Wooden's first hoop was not a peach basket, but a tomato basket. His first ball was not a soccer ball, but bunched rags stuffed into one of his mother's stockings. Unlike Naismith, Wooden didn't start the basketball craze. But, as UCLA's basketball coach, he started a certain kind of basketball insanity in Los Angeles, California.

In the town of Martinsville, Indiana, Wooden was All-State high school player for three straight years, then consensus All-American at Purdue for three years after that. Like other players from the

Many great stars of the NBA learned from the best coach in college basketball history: John Wooden of UCLA.

early days of basketball, he might have turned pro had it been possible to make a good living playing ball.

After years spent coaching in the Midwest, Wooden accepted the head coaching job at UCLA in 1948. He was a gifted teacher who specialized in a fast-break style. His string of successes started in the 1960s, but really took off when a young New Yorker known as Lew Alcindor (the young Kareem Abdul-Jabbar) decided to attend college in California.

After Abdul-Jabbar graduated to the NBA, Wooden and the UCLA Bruins were joined by Bill Walton. Walton was a big colorful shooter, passer, and rebounder who led the 1977 Portland Trail Blazers to their only world championship. Although his career was cut short by continuing injuries and a bad foot, he was successful at UCLA. Under Wooden's leadership, Walton and the Bruins racked up 88 consecutive wins and two more NCAA Championships.

When Wooden finally retired he had led the Bruins to ten national championships in his last 12 years as coach. It will be a while before that record is ever topped.

Bill Sharman—Elected 1974

A fearless competitor and highly skilled shooter, Bill Sharman became the first player to sink more than 50 *free throws* in a row (a one-point shot taken from the free-throw line). He is still the only player to have three streaks of making 50 or more free throws in a row. During his 11-year career, he won the free-throw shooting title seven times, and made fully 88 percent of the free throws he attempted. Along with Rick Barry and Larry Bird, Sharman was one of the finest free throw shooters ever to step to the foul line.

After retiring, he coached the Cleveland Pipers in the ABL, the Utah Stars in the ABA, and the L.A.

Lakers in the NBA. When he became the Lakers' coach in the early 1970s, he introduced "the morning meeting," a pregame practice now called the *shootaround*. When the Lakers were successful, every team in the league introduced its own shootaround. It became a part of pregame routine in the NBA. Unfortunately, the stresses of coaching proved too much for his voice, and Sharman had to step down as Laker coach. Named General Manager of the Lakers in 1980, he became president of the team in 1985. When he was elected to the Hall of Fame in 1974, he was the only member to hold ten championship basketball rings in three different leagues (ABL, ABA, and NBA).

Red Auerbach—Elected 1968

Baseball's feisty Leo Durocher once remarked that, "nice guys finish last." Celtics coach Red Auerbach offered his own variation. "Show me a good loser," he said, "and I'll show you a loser." Like Durocher, Auerbach had a way of communicating his own desire to win to his players and, in case they doubted, to referees. When things didn't go his way, he tore his hair, punched things, screamed at refs, and even flicked cigar ashes at them. Short, stocky, and balding, Auerbach had a lot of sass for the referees and a big cigar he liked to light up to taunt his opponents whenever he believed the Celtics had secured a win.

As Boston's coach during the Bill Russell era, Auerbach was not a particularly good loser. To his credit and the credit of the great players who played for him, however, he didn't have to be. During his years of coaching he amassed 938 victories, suffered only 479 losses, and led Boston to nine NBA Championships. This doesn't give him the highest winning percentage of any coach, but it does give him the greatest number of victories in the NBA. After he stepped down as coach,

*The greatest all-black basketball team in history was the New
York Renaissance, honored by the Hall of Fame in 1963.*

his influence behind the scenes continued as the Celtics
hoisted five more championship flags. Today Auerbach
is President of the Boston Celtics.

The New York Renaissance—Elected 1963

Jackie Robinson broke the so-called "color line" in
baseball when he joined the Brooklyn Dodgers in 1947
and became the first African-American to play major
league baseball. Basketball was a little slower to
integrate. It wasn't until 1950 that the Boston Celtics

integrated professional basketball by drafting Chuck Cooper. The New York Knicks soon followed suit by acquiring Nate "Sweetwater" Clifton from the Harlem Globetrotters, a team of traveling basketball clowns. Prior to 1950, African-American players were unwelcome in professional basketball. If used at all, they were allowed to play on a limited basis in college. To deal with this racism, black players formed their own teams and traveled the country taking on any and all teams who would play them.

The New York Renaissance was a team formed in New York City and named after a Harlem casino and nightclub. The "Rens" took to the road in 1922, traveling and playing wherever they could for more than 20 years. Because of widespread racism and suspicion, the Rens were routinely denied hotel rooms and restaurant service. They often ate their meals on trains, slept in their own cars, or stayed in private homes. But nobody worked harder at basketball. They traveled constantly by car and train and played as many as 130 games a year.

Despite hardships and hostility, the Rens won more than 100 games over their last 14 years. In 1939 for instance, they were 112-7. Before breaking up in the 1940s, they had built up a record of 2,588 wins and 529 losses. In 1933, they beat the original Celtics team seven out of eight games. The Renaissance were a worthy foe for any team in the country.

When Wilt Chamberlain entered the NBA, his height and agility made him an instant star as he broke records in shooting and rebounding.

Sixties Stars

As teams became accustomed to the 24-second shot clock in the mid-1950s, the faster pace of the game made it more exciting to watch, and television began broadcasting more professional games. It was during this period that some of the greatest players ever began entering the league. They were skillful passers and great shooters. Among them were Hall of Fame members such as Dolph Schayes, Bob Cousy, Bob Pettit, Elgin Baylor, Oscar Robertson, and Bill Russell. And then there was a giant who was responsible for changing the sport all by himself.

Wilt Chamberlain—Elected 1978

Neither Kareem Abdul-Jabbar nor Michael Jordan ever managed to dominate basketball the way Wilt Chamberlain once did. And he did it in a league dense with other great players such as Jerry West, John Havlicek, and Bob Cousy. Chamberlain may well have been the greatest basketball player to date.

During his career, the league made no less than three rule changes in an attempt to reduce his impact on the sport. He liked to jump up and shoot his free throws from the air. That was banned. Next, the league adopted *goaltending* rules that forced Chamberlain to change his style of offensive play under the boards. And finally, the inbound pass over the backboard was banned to keep him from enjoying the full advantage of his height. Even so, there was no stopping the man known to his fans as "Wilt the Stilt" and "the Dipper."

Shadowed by basketball scouts from the day he

entered high school, Chamberlain was recruited from Philadelphia's Overbrook High to play for the University of Kansas. When he finally signed to play with the Philadelphia Warriors, he led the league in scoring (field goals) his first year. He would eventually lead the league in field goals seven times and in field goal average nine times. Arguably, he was an even better rebounder than a shooter, leading the league in rebounding 11 times during his 14 years as a pro. He pulled down no fewer than 23,924 career rebounds—about 2,000 more than second-place Bill Russell and 5,000 more than third-place Abdul-Jabbar. His average of 23 has only been approached in recent years by one player: Dennis Rodman.

Shooting? Although Abdul-Jabbar leads Chamberlain in many categories, including years played and total field goals, Abdul-Jabbar had a much lower scoring average than that of Chamberlain. Only superstar Michael Jordan has a comparable field goal average.

Finally, despite his size and toughness, Chamberlain almost never fouled out of games. He couldn't shoot free throws very well, and was not always aggressive when it came to covering his man on defense, but he is still probably the greatest basketball player of all time.

Oscar Robertson—Elected 1979

Among NBA stars, only Abdul-Jabbar, Chamberlain, and Elvin Hayes have bettered Oscar Robertson's total of 26,710 points. During his 14-year career, the six-foot, five-inch Robertson averaged a remarkable 25.7 points per game. And with 9,887, he's second in all-time assists to Magic Johnson. Until surpassed recently by the long-playing Moses Malone, Robertson held the all-time free throw record with

Oscar Robertson was a star in college who became one of the NBA's premier play-makers. He is second in career assists after Magic Johnson.

7,694. Robertson obviously belongs front and center in any discussion about the greatest players of all time.

Wilt Chamberlain, whose career lasted about as long as Robertson's, overshadowed him in scoring and rebounding. But Robertson was a better free-throw shooter, had a higher free-throw shooting percentage, and had more than twice as many assists. According to Abdul-Jabbar, the man known in basketball as "the Big O" was one of the best passers ever to pick up a basketball. Robertson's game was based on his ability to get a step on anybody guarding him. Then he either beat his defender to the basket, drew extra defenders and whipped off a pass to a teammate, or drove for the basket—sometimes managing to get fouled even as he made the basket.

Abdul-Jabbar wrote, "Oscar had whole seasons

where he averaged triple-double stats for the entire year (points, assists, rebounds). Such dominance from someone in the guard position was not fully appreciated in those days." UCLA Coach John Wooden said that the real measure of Robertson's greatness was that he always "first looked for the pass."

Jerry West—Elected 1979

Can you imagine a regular-season NBA team that included Michael Jordan, Larry Bird, and Karl Malone? Unbeatable? Maybe, but in 1968 the Los Angeles Lakers had a team that might have beaten them. They had Wilt Chamberlain, Elgin Baylor, and Jerry West—three of the top ten NBA scorers of all time. Unlucky for the Lakers and lucky for the Celtics and the rest of the NBA, Chamberlain, Baylor, and West were rarely all healthy and playing their best at the same time. Cotton Fitzsimmons, coach of the Phoenix Suns, especially raved about West. "He has the hands of a safecracker," he said.

Known for his shooting, West was a sparkling defender as well. He was especially good at ball stealing and passing. Although he was teamed with Chamberlain and Baylor, West probably had more in common with Oscar Robertson. Both were born in 1938, played in the NBA for 14 years, retired in 1974, and were elected to the Hall of Fame in 1975. They were about the same size, played together on the 1960 Olympic team, averaged better than 25 points a game, hit better than 80 percent from the free-throw line, and eventually entered the elite among scorers with more than 25,000 points.

Have you ever looked closely at the NBA logo? The outline of the player on it is Jerry West. After retiring, West went on to coach the Lakers, then moved up to the position of general manager, a position he continues to hold today.

Bill Russell—Elected 1974

At six-feet, nine-inches, Bill Russell was a college standout who led the University of San Francisco to two NCAA Championships and 60 straight victories in the 1950s. Still, few people thought Russell would make it in the pros because his shooting was only so-so. Celtic coach Red Auerbach, however, told Russell that he didn't care if he ever scored. What he wanted was defense. With Russell on the court, Auerbach got that and then some.

Russell brought a new, highly mobile style of defensive play to basketball. His opponents were never quite sure where he was. There is no record of how many shots he blocked in his career, because the NBA didn't keep track of blocked shots until several years after he retired. But without a doubt he was among the very best defensive players in the history of the game.

Today, many NBA stars can't resist the temptation to show off or humiliate opponents by slam-blocking shots. The problem with this tactic is that the ball often goes out of bounds afterward, and possession then reverts back to the team that had its shot blocked. Russell was careful to block shots only hard enough to make sure they'd miss. Then he'd try to claim possession of the ball.

Russell is the best answer to the question, "How important is defense?" The Celtics were a high-scoring team before Russell joined them, but they were always eliminated in the playoffs. With Russell's arrival, the Celtics became virtually unbeatable, accomplishing a feat never done before or since: They won 11 of 13 NBA championships. Bill Russell was the only Celtic player who played on each of those 11 world championship teams.

For a time before going into retirement, Russell served as a player/manager for the Celtics. In 1973, he

Bill Russell was the game's best defensive center throughout the dynasty years of the Boston Celtics. Many fans consider him the best center ever.

took over the Seattle Supersonics franchise as both coach and general manager, becoming the first African-American player to reach that high into professional basketball management.

Arnold "Red" Holzman—Elected 1985

During his years of play, this former Rochester, New York, hoopster and New York Knicks coach acquired enough plaques and rings to open a small jewelry store. He was given his first ring for playing on the championship Rochester Royals team of 1946, and he earned two rings for coaching the New York Knicks to championships in 1970 and 1972. Two more rings came his way for coaching two NBA All-Star Teams, and he received another ring for coaching the NBA Legends Game. His seventh ring was given him when he was elected to the Basketball Hall of Fame in 1985. Holzman said this ring was the most important.

Holzman is the only person in NBA history to have coached in four decades. He is the only player, scout, coach, and general manager to be active in five different decades. His greatest year may have been in 1970, when his underdog New York Knicks captured the city's first NBA Championship from a Laker team that included Wilt Chamberlain, Jerry West, and Elgin Baylor. Holzman still serves as a consultant to the Knicks.

Elgin Baylor—Elected 1976

Even though Wilt Chamberlain cast a tall shadow during Elgin Baylor's prime playing years, this great forward was able to escape from and even thrive outside that mighty shadow. While Bill Russell led the Celtics to world championships and Chamberlain broke record after record for scoring and rebounding, Baylor pounded up and down the court posting *triple doubles* night after night (that is, scoring more than ten points, pulling

Elgin Baylor prepares to throw down another basket. This great forward spent his entire career with the Minneapolis and Los Angeles Lakers.

down more than ten rebounds, and making more than ten assists).

After a college career in Seattle, Baylor played with the Minneapolis Lakers in 1958-59. During his rookie year he was fourth in points scored, ninth in assists, and third in rebounds. His second year, with an average of 29.6 points per game, he was third in scoring. The next year he was second-best in scoring. He never led the league in scoring or rebounding, yet he was always among the leaders. As long as he was a Laker (in Minneapolis and Los Angeles), his team was always in contention for a world championship.

Tenth in all-time scoring after a 14-year career, Baylor is second only to Wilt Chamberlain in points per game with a sensational 27.4 average. Not as accurate as either Kareem or Chamberlain, Baylor was still indisputably among the best of the best. He is one of ten players with more than 10,000 rebounds and more than 20,000 points. Only at the very end of his career did the Lakers manage to win a world championship. Shortly thereafter, Baylor retired.

No one excited basketball fans during the 1970s like Julius Erving. "Dr. J"
played several years in the short-lived ABA before bringing his high-flying style
to Philadelphia—and a championship to the 76ers.

Seventies Supermen

T he original NBA consisted of ten teams, organized into an Eastern and a Western Division. But in 1967, the NBA faced a major challenge. A group of businessmen formed the American Basketball Association (ABA). The ABA introduced the *three-point* shot. The ABA hoped that three-point opportunities would improve player shooting skills and lead to higher-scoring games. They believed this would draw even more fans. Smaller men who were good three-point shooters now had a chance to compete against the big slam-dunkers like Chamberlain and Abdul-Jabbar.

Eventually the ABA folded after a few years. Its stars were recruited by an expanded NBA, and professional basketball was bigger than ever. A new crop of stars emerged in the 1970s.

Elvin Hayes—Elected 1989

At the tender age of 8, Elvin Hayes went to work in the cotton fields near Rayville, Louisiana. This left him little time for sports. And his equipment wasn't that hot, either. His first basketball was a rolled up sock that he would lob through a loop of scrap metal nailed to a tree—a rough beginning for a smooth player. But the "Big E" went on to become the third leading scorer in NBA history.

After an impressive college career with the

University of Houston, Hayes signed with the San Diego Rockets. The six-foot, nine-inch center led the league in scoring during his rookie year with a 28-point average. Although he never won the scoring title again, he placed among the top scorers year after year until the twilight of his career. As good as he was, fate was not particularly kind to him. Hayes played for several losing or mediocre teams, and so he was often overlooked by the media.

Hayes played on only one world championship team, the 1977-78 Washington Bullets. Year after year, he was elected to the All-Star team, but was never named Most Valuable Player. When he retired in 1984, he was near the top of the heap in scoring and rebounding, and had more playing time (some 50,000 minutes) than any other player in NBA history. But Abdul-Jabbar took even that record away from him by playing for several more years after Hayes quit. It's interesting to speculate what would have happened if Hayes had played on more winning teams during his career.

Bill Bradley—Elected 1982

Henry David Thoreau was a 19th-century American writer who stressed individualism, or what he called the importance of marching to the beat of your own drummer. Thoreau's favorite basketball player would probably have been Bill Bradley.

Princeton University is not known for its winning basketball teams, but Bill Bradley wasn't bothered by that. A brilliant student, he chose to get the best possible education and accepted an academic rather than an athletic scholarship. He spent his summers trying to improve living conditions for the American poor, working for the Urban League's Street Academy in Harlem and for the Office of Economic Opportunity in

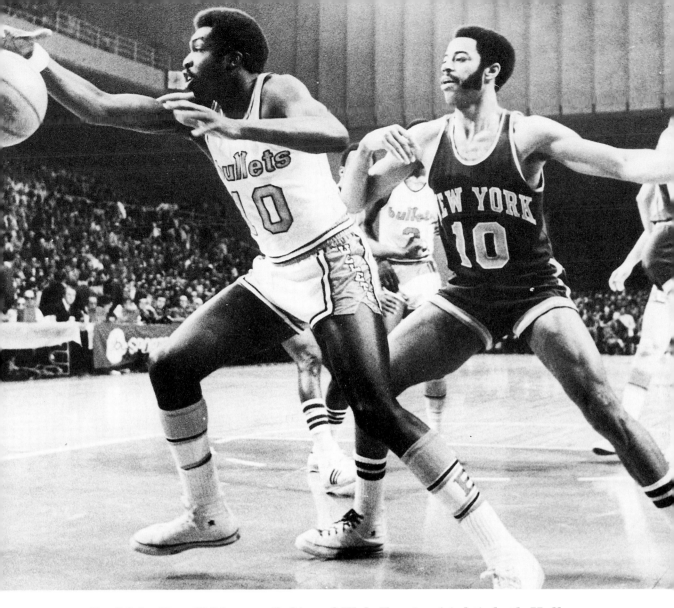

Earl "the Pearl" Monroe (left) and Walt Frazier (right), both Hall of Famers, played many great years in the NBA during the 1970s.

Washington, D.C. Following his outstanding academic and basketball career at Princeton, Bradley passed up offers to play professional ball to attend Oxford University in England as a Rhodes Scholar. After completing his education, he became a spirited team player for the New York Knicks' championship teams of 1970 and 1972.

Although he never led the league in any category, he was the ultimate team player and served as a team leader wherever he played. Following his retirement from basketball, Bradley became involved in politics. He is now a United States Senator from New Jersey.

Pete Maravich—Elected 1987

Hair that flopped when he jumped, baggy socks that fell down around his ankles, and a jump shot among the game's best: These were the trademarks of "Pistol" Pete Maravich, one of the showiest basketball gunslingers ever to don an NBA uniform. The son of Press Maravich, who played for the Pittsburgh Ironmen in the early days of the league, Pete learned to dribble by age three and balance a basketball on one finger by the time he was eight. As a teenager, he took a basketball to the movies and dribbled in the aisles.

Eventually, Pete went to Louisiana State University where, coached by his father, he acquired his reputation as a scoring machine. He was the leading college scorer three years in a row. In 1968-69, he broke college scoring records with a 44.2 point average and 1,148 points. As a senior he improved his scoring average to 44.5 points per game. Something of a showoff, Maravich was known to dribble behind his back, make fancy passes unnecessarily, and generally enjoy himself on the court. Because his career had been so carefully managed in college, he was famous before he ever arrived in the NBA.

In the NBA he was a bigger star than any of his teammates and most of the other league players. In March 1970 he signed a five-year contract with the Atlanta Hawks. After four years with the Hawks, during which he averaged about 23 points a game, Maravich was traded to the New Orleans Jazz. He led the NBA in scoring in 1976-77 with a 31.1 average for New Orleans, but had rather an erratic, injury-prone career. After a decade of play, he retired. He was a player with hot nights and hot streaks, and those who

"Pistol" Pete Maravich was one of the most exciting shooters in
the NBA. His flashy dribbling and pinpoint jump shots made him
a favorite at Jazz games.

Elvin Hayes (left) labored long and hard for several pro teams to become the sixth-leading scorer in combined ABA-NBA history.

saw him when he was hot won't forget him any time soon. Tragically, Maravich collapsed after a pickup game many years later, and died before he was 50.

Rick Barry—Elected 1987

Call him Mr. Free Throw. Barry was the most successful shooter ever to toe the line for the NBA. He launched his free throws underhand with a deadly spin and flick of the wrist. Moses Malone is the all-time free throw king in terms of total points (8,000 and rising), but Malone enjoyed a long career of getting fouled every night. His average, however, is about 10 percentage points lower than Barry's.

In fact, from a free-throw percentage standpoint, Barry is matchless. During his 14-year career, he attempted 6,397 free throws and made 5,713. This gives him an average of 89.3 percent, slightly above that posted by Calvin Murphy and significantly higher than those posted by current free-throw marksmen Larry Bird (88.4 percent) or Chris Mullin (88 percent). The closeness of these percentage points, however, is deceiving. By comparison, Mullin is just getting started, and Barry made about 2,000 more free throws than either Murphy or Bird. During the 1978-79 season, Barry posted a free-throw percentage of .947, establishing an all-time NBA record for free-throw accuracy that still stands.

Like Julius Erving and many other great players, Barry began his 14-year career in the ABA, where he was an aggressive forward who was never afraid to contest a referee's call. If he's credited for points he scored in both leagues, Barry is 11th on the list of all-time leading scorers.

Kareem Abdul-Jabbar is the game's all-time leading scorer, with more than 38,000 points.

Future Members?

Each year thousands of talented high school athletes are given a chance to prove themselves on college basketball courts. Of the thousands, perhaps 40 are drafted by the NBA and given a chance to show they can play basketball with the biggest and the best. Of the 40, a dozen will probably survive the competition and go on to enjoy productive careers in the NBA. Fewer still play long enough and with teams successful enough, to have any impact on the professional game.

Yet the question is asked each season: Who will be the next Wilt Chamberlain, Bill Russell, or Magic Johnson? It's a question of continuing interest to fans, coaches, players, corporate sponsors, and referees. Since the Hall of Fame now requires that there be five new members elected every year, any NBA player with a long and productive career has a good chance of making it.

Kareem Abdul-Jabbar—Retired 1989

It would be easier to take the salt out of a box of popcorn than to remove Abdul-Jabbar's name from basketball record books. A thinking man who liked to read a book to clear his mind before a game, Kareem was a unique player. His shot was the *skyhook,* an unstoppable toss that won game after game for the Lakers. "Doctor J," also known as Julius Erving, called him "the greatest basketball player of all time." Since Erving himself is surely one of the greatest basketball players of all time, that's quite a compliment.

It's hard to find anything new to write about the seven-foot center who stood under the Laker basket and dominated the game for 20 years. But if 500 years from now anybody is interested in the first century of basketball, Kareem's name will be everywhere. In this age of statistics, his records could fill a medium-sized book. The object in basketball is to score points, and of the thousands who've played in the pros, Kareem scored more points than anybody. In fact, with his 38,387 points, he racked up about 7,000 more points than Chamberlain, his nearest rival. There are no active NBA players closer than 12,000 points to his record. Larry Bird will not come close. And if Michael Jordan is ever to break it, he will have to play and score at his current clip for about ten more years.

Yet there was more to Kareem than the points he scored. He's the all-time leader in field goal percentage, which simply means that he wasted fewer shots. Kareem is the all-time leader in games played. Appearing in 18 All-Star games, he was named to 15 all-NBA teams and was voted NBA MVP six times. He's second in rebounds behind Chamberlain, and led the league in blocked shots on four different occasions. When he's finally elected to the Hall of Fame, they may have to give him a room of his own.

Michael Jordan—Rookie year 1985

Michael Jordan is everywhere these days: on the basketball court, television, posters, T-shirts, cereal boxes, and magazine covers. It's hard to believe he was once so thoroughly overlooked.

Jordan was cut from his high school team as a sophomore in South Carolina, and passed over by those

Many fans expect Michael Jordan to be a Hall of Fame member in his first year of eligibility.

selecting All-America high school basketball stars. He wasn't even invited to play in any of the high school All-Star tournaments.

Coming out of college, Jordan didn't know whether he could make it in the NBA. But almost from the beginning, he convinced fans that he was one of the greatest athletes to ever play basketball. As a guard of the Chicago Bulls, he has compiled the highest scoring average of any player in the history of the league (32.6). He is still a long way from records set by Chamberlain, Abdul-Jabbar, and Robertson, but whatever happens in the future, Jordan has a round-trip, champagne-class ticket to the Basketball Hall of Fame any time he wants it. Will he be the greatest basketball player of all time? Most fans think he's well on his way.

Larry Bird—Rookie year 1980

In 1982, former Boston Celtics great and Hall of Famer Bob Cousy said, "Everybody is going to say it in five years, but I'm going to say it now. Larry Bird is the greatest player ever to play this foolish game." As it happened, Cousy had not yet heard of a player named Michael Jordan. Five years later, in 1987, so many fans were saying Jordan was the greatest player that many began to forget that Indiana-born Boston Celtic named Bird.

But speed, grace, and flash are not everything. Larry Bird proved that game after game, long before Jordan joined the Bulls, and he's still proving it. There isn't anything that puts points on the scoreboard that the six-foot, nine-inch Bird doesn't do and hasn't done for the Celtics for 12 years. He is one of just 15 players in NBA history ever to score more than 20,000 points, and one of nine players to have averaged more than 24 points per game for more than 10 years. Furthermore, he's made better than 88 percent of his free throws, which makes him one of the best free-throw shooters ever to step to the line.

For the last dozen years Bird has averaged about 10 rebounds per game. And with the recent retirement of NBA record-holder Magic Johnson, Bird now leads all active NBA players in assists. If sweeping the floor before the game would help the Celtics win, he'd be the first one out there with a broom. One day Bird will walk into the Hall of Fame on a thick red carpet.

Magic Johnson—Retired 1991

The one and only founder of "Showtime," Earvin Johnson was the ultimate ball handler and floor reader. He could see patterns and openings that hadn't yet developed. From 1980 until he retired early in the 1991-92 season, Johnson's career nicely compared with that of

Larry Bird's great career with one team, the Celtics, has brought him three MVP awards—and three championships to Boston.

Larry Bird, who came into the league at the same time. Bird racked up more total points, but Johnson had greater accuracy and scored with a higher percentage of his shots. From the free-throw line it was reversed. Magic had more free throws, since a ball-handling guard is typically fouled more often. But Bird made more of the free throws he was awarded. Taller and positioned inside, Bird also had the advantage in rebounding numbers.

The difference—in fact the difference between Magic and any active player—was that the Magic show was really about assists, and blinding, unbelievable passes. Only Oscar Robertson found as many ways of helping his teammates score, and Magic surpassed even Robertson. "He determines in an instant how a play might develop, and can automatically make the most of slight, fleeting advantages," wrote Johnson's teammate, Kareem Abdul-Jabbar. Magic's ability to "see the whole court" was rated second to none.

Most fans believe that Magic's presence on the Lakers teams of the 1980s changed the modern game of basketball. From a game once dominated by tall, lumbering centers, basketball has become a game dominated by agile point guards like Johnson who are ready, willing, and able to do it all. One day soon Magic will be Alley-Ooped into the Hall of Fame.

Julius Erving—Retired 1987

Atlanta Hawk Dominique Wilkins may be known as "the Human Highlight Film," but before Wilkins, the television sports moments were provided by "Doctor J." At six-feet, six-inches, Julius Erving was not a big man by basketball standards, but he became a dazzling player. He had an amazing ability to propel himself through the air, and he seemed to stay up there longer.

Once when Erving was asked how he managed to

dunk the ball in so many different ways and from so many different positions, he replied, "It's easy once you learn how to fly." He could also hold the ball in one hand, much like a softball. His trademark move was a drive around his defender, a long leap from outside the free-throw line, a sail of 15 feet or more to the basket, and then a deep stuff of the ball.

Erving grew up on Long Island and, like Chamberlain, Abdul-Jabbar, Willis Reed, or Connie Hawkins, spent a lot of time practicing his moves in the school yard. After attending the University of Massachusets for a time, he joined the Virginia Squires, an ABA team. Word of Erving's skills spread even though TV paid little attention to the ABA. He averaged 27 points a game in his rookie year. His second year, he led the new league in scoring with an average of 32 points per game. Soon he was among the leaders in all ABA categories. When the ABA folded, Erving was snatched into the NBA by the Philadelphia 76ers.

Millions of people who had never seen him in the ABA became basketball fans just by watching the Doctor drive and stuff. Erving helped lead the 76ers to the playoffs in nine out of 11 seasons. Erving kept them in contention year after year until they won the 1982-83 finals with Moses Malone to help. When his totals in the ABA are combined with his NBA stats, he becomes the third-highest scorer in the history of the game, with a total of 30,026 points scored over 16 years.

Moses Malone—Rookie year 1977

In 1974, when Moses Malone was a high school senior, more than 300 people offered him advice about which college to choose. Moses, who could—and still can—jump like an antelope, led his high school team in Petersburg, Virginia, to 50 victories without a loss. He averaged 36 points, 25 rebounds, and 10 blocked shots per game. Then he went to college, but not for long. After just one day at the University of Maryland, Malone hooked up with the Utah Stars, an ABA team. At 19, Malone became the youngest player ever to break into professional basketball.

As young players often do, Moses ran into trouble. The ABA was a long way from high school. Shooting, passing, and ball handling while surrounded by experienced players was overwhelming at first, but Malone soon showed that he was going to prevail and be among the best rebounders in basketball history. His first year in the ABA, he averaged 18 points and grabbed more than 1,200 rebounds. When the ABA merged with the NBA, Moses played a couple of games for Buffalo before joining the Houston Rockets. That year he was third in rebounding. The following year, despite missing almost 25 games, he was second in rebounding. He once led the league in rebounding for five years straight—a streak even Chamberlain never matched.

Malone spent his most productive years with Houston and Philadelphia, becoming one of the top scorers of all time—surpassing 29,000 points. A big man with a powerful inside game, he has burned a hole in the free-throw circle, making well over 8,000. He holds the record for playing 1,047 games without fouling out. Recently traded to the Milwaukee Bucks, Malone is not far from retirement and a berth in the Basketball Hall of Fame.

Basketball's All-Time Best Players

Year listed is when each member was inducted.

Nate Archibald	1991	Sam Jones	1983
Paul Arizin	1977	Edward Krause	1975
Thomas Barlow	1980	Bob Kurland	1961
Rick Barry	1987	Joe Lapchick	1966
Elgin Baylor	1976	Clyde Lovellette	1988
John Beckman	1972	Jerry Lucas	1979
Dave Bing	1990	Hank Luisetti	1959
Benny Borgmann	1961	Ed Macauley	1960
Bill Bradley	1982	Pete Maravich	1987
Joe Brennan	1974	Slater Martin	1981
Al Cervi	1984	Branch McCracken	1960
Wilt Chamberlain	1978	Jack McCracken	1962
Charles Cooper	1976	Bobby McDermott	1988
Bob Cousy	1970	George Mikan	1959
Dave Cowens	1991	Earl Monroe	1990
Billy Cunningham	1986	Charles Murphy	1960
Bob Davies	1969	Harlan Page	1962
Forrest DeBernardi	1961	Bob Pettit	1970
Dave DeBusschere	1982	Andy Phillip	1961
Dutch Dehnert	1968	Jim Pollard	1977
Paul Endacott	1971	Frank Ramsey	1981
Bud Foster	1964	Willis Reed	1981
Walt Frazier	1987	Oscar Robertson	1979
Marty Friedman	1971	John Roosma	1961
Joe Fulks	1977	John Russell	1964
Laddie Gale	1976	Bill Russell	1974
Harry Gallatin	1991	Dolph Schayes	1972
William Gates	1989	Ernest J. Schmidt	1973
Tom Gola	1975	John Schommer	1959
Hal Greer	1981	Barney Sedran	1962
Robert Gruenig	1963	Bill Sharman	1975
Cliff Hagan	1977	Christian Steinmetz	1961
Victor Hanson	1960	John Thompson	1962
John Havlicek	1983	Nate Thurmond	1984
Elvin Hayes	1990	Jack Twyman	1982
Tom Heinsohn	1986	Wes Unseld	1988
Nat Holman	1964	Robert Vandivier	1974
Bob Houbregs	1987	Ed Wachter	1961
Chuck Hyatt	1959	Bobby Wanzer	1987
Bill Johnson	1976	Jerry West	1979
Neil Johnston	1990	Lenny Wilkens	1989
K.C. Jones	1989	John Wooden	1960

Glossary

ASSISTS. When a player makes a pass to a teammate that results in a field goal or basket.

FREE THROW. A one-point play made when a player attempts a basket from the free-throw line after being fouled.

GOALTENDING. When a player blocks a shot as it descends toward the basket. This is now illegal.

REBOUNDS. Grabbing the basketball after it bounces off either the offensive or defensive backboard.

SHOOTAROUND. A common NBA practice session before the start of a game.

THREE-POINT SHOT. A basket that earns a team three points (instead of two) when shot from behind the three-point line.

TRIPLE DOUBLE. When a player scores at least 10 points, grabs at least 10 rebounds, and makes at least 10 assists in a single game.

24-SECOND SHOT CLOCK. A team must attempt a basket within a 24-second time limit, or else the opposing team gets possession of the ball.

Bibliography

Aaseng, Nathan. *Basketball's High Flyers.* Minneapolis: Lerner Publications, 1980.

Abdul-Jabbar, Kareem with Mignon McCarthy. *Kareem.* New York: Random House, 1990.

Axthelm, Peter. *The City Game.* New York: Harper's Magazine Press, 1970.

Bird, Larry with John Bischoff. *Bird On Basketball.* Reading, Massachusetts: Addison-Wesley, 1983.

Fox, Larry. *The Illustrated History Of Basketball.* Long Island City, New York: Grosset & Dunlap, 1974.

Goldpaper and Pincus. *How To Talk Basketball.* New York: Dembner Books, 1983.

Holzman, Red and Harvey Frommer. *Red On Red.* New York: Bantam, 1987.

Jarrett, William S. *Timetables Of Sports History.* New York: Facts on File, 1990.

Kerr, Johnny and Terry Pluto. *Bull Session.* Chicago: Bonus Books, 1989.

Salzberg, Charles. *From Set Shot To Slam Dunk.* New York: E.P. Dutton, 1987.

Shaughnessy, Dan. *Ever Green.* New York: St. Martin's Press, 1990.

The Sporting News Official NBA Guide, 1991-92. St. Louis: The Sporting News, 1991.

Wolff, Alexander and Armen Keteyian. *Raw Recruits.* New York: Pocket Books, 1990.

Photo Credits

ALLSPORT USA: 4 (Rick Stewart); 8, 36 (Mike Powell); 39 (Tim DeFrisco); 41 (D. Strohmeyer)
Basketball Hall of Fame: 7, 10, 13 (Hickox Library), 16
Wide World Photos: 18, 21, 24, 26, 28, 31, 33, 34

Index